Family in Cree/English

By Sylvia Caribou

Copyright © 2017 Sylvia Caribou

All rights reserved. No portion of this book may be reproduced in any form without permission from the publisher, except as permitted by Canadian and U.S.A. copyright law. For permissions contact Sylvia Caribou

The advice and strategies found within may not be suitable for every situation. This work is sold with the understanding that neither the author nor the publisher are held responsible for the results accrued from the advice in this book.

ISBN-13: 978-0-9958408-3-6

DEDICATION

Especially to my dear parents Mr. Adam Castel and Mrs. Domithilde Castel. Friends and family. My hope is that you take care of each other, love one another, you and your family. Teaching your child how to love and grow up to be a good citizen is very important.

Kethawow oma ochi Takiskiseyek

Oma mena emasinahikestamawakwak ninekihikwak niwwechiwakanak ekwa nichisanak, nitotemak. Ni pakosithemon ta manachihitowek asichi ta sakihitowek mena tamanatchihitowek. Ta kisinahamawachik kichawasimisinawak ekwa tasakehitochick ekwa mena tanisitotakwa manachihitowin eta actaskechik

Thanks also to Cornelius Bighetty for this translation work and to the staff of the Pukatawagan Regional Centre, University College of the North, Ralph Caribou, Coordinator, and Janice Seto, Instructor of the Diploma Community Economic Development program.

Family walks 2017

Grand-Nieces and Nephews

Netotemak ekwa nestesak, nimesak ochawasimisewawa napisisak ekwa mena eskwesisak

Grand-Mothers Mrs Moon and Therese Bighetty

Ko-Ko-minack

My Puppies
Nitcheemisisak

Dad Adam, brother Eli, Sylvia, brother Keith and my Mom Domithilde Castel

Notawiy, nistesack ekwa netha asiche nikawiy

Mom, Dad, Sister in Laws-Sandra and Cathy

Nekaweyak, Notawiy ekwa Nikawiy asicki Nichakosak

Sisters and brother in law Nimisak akwa nestaw Ekwa nistes Stan

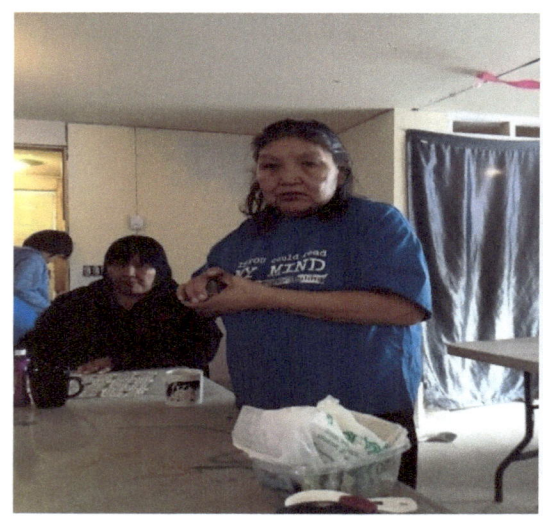

Brothers, Sister Nisteesak ekwa nemis

Grand-Sons and Grand-Daughter

Nosisemak, napisisak ekwa eskwesis

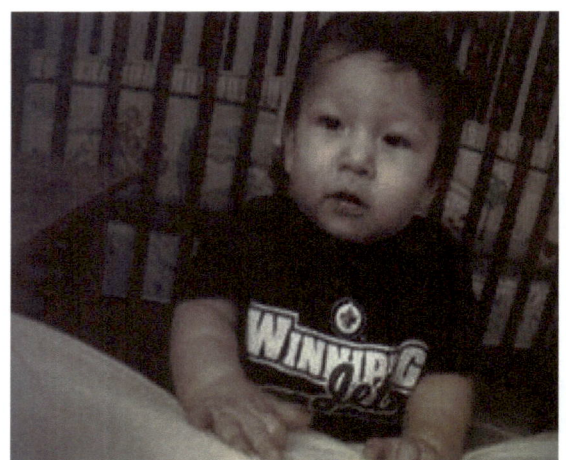

Grand-Daughter Aleia

Nosisem, eskwesis Aleia

Uncle Wally

Nokomish Wally

Grand-Nieces and Nephews

Nitotimak ochawasimiswawa Reanna, Billy ekwa wetapiskonakan Billy okosisa

Nephews and me

Nitotemak ekwa netha

Nieces and Daughters

Nitotemak ekwa netha neso okok ota anokosichik nichanisak

Nieces and Nephews and grand-nephew

Nimes ekwa nistes ochawasimiseewawa ekwa kotak nitapiskonakan

Brother in Law, Sister and Cousin

Nestaw ekwa nimis, nestaw kotak john ekwa netotem ernest

Sister in law and Brothers

Nistes Eli ekwa Nichakos Shirely

Nistes Peter ekwa Nichakos Geraldine

Son-in-law, daughter and grandson

Nitekwatem ekwa, Nosisem ekwa Nichanes

Son-in-Law, daughter and grand-daughter

Nitekwatem Charlie, Nichanis Yolanda, ekwa Nosisem Aliea

Sisters, Sister-in-laws, and Cousins

Nimisak ekwa Netha, Nichakos Shirley ekwa Nitotimak asiche Nichanis

My son's, Nikosisak

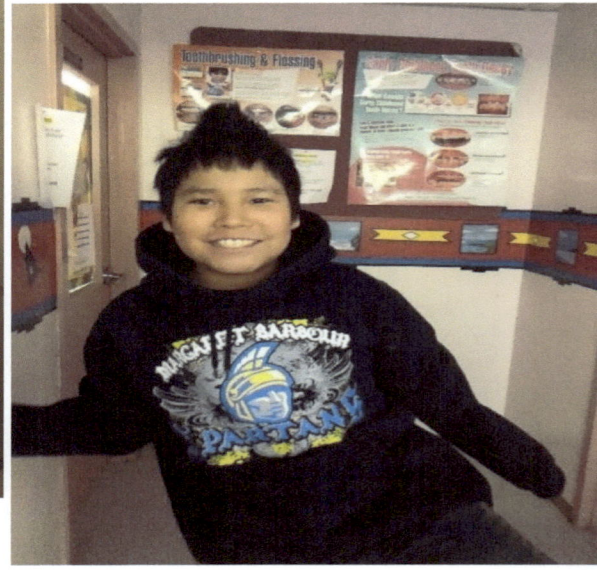

Cousins

Nikosisak Ototema

Grand-son, grand-nephews

Nosisem Corbin ekwa, Netotemak okosisiwawa

Grand-Nephews and Nephews

Nistes ochawasisima, ekwa oskiawasis Evan

Grand-Sons
Nosisimak

Nephew Steven and Family

Nistes okosisa Steven ekwa owekimakana Coreen asichi ochawasimisa

Famous Pukatawagan sign

Pakitohokani

Nephew/Cousins/Brother

Nistes okosisa, Thomas, Nitotemak Tyrone ekwa Verna asichi Nistes Richard, omisis asichi esithekasot J.R Kapatahohket

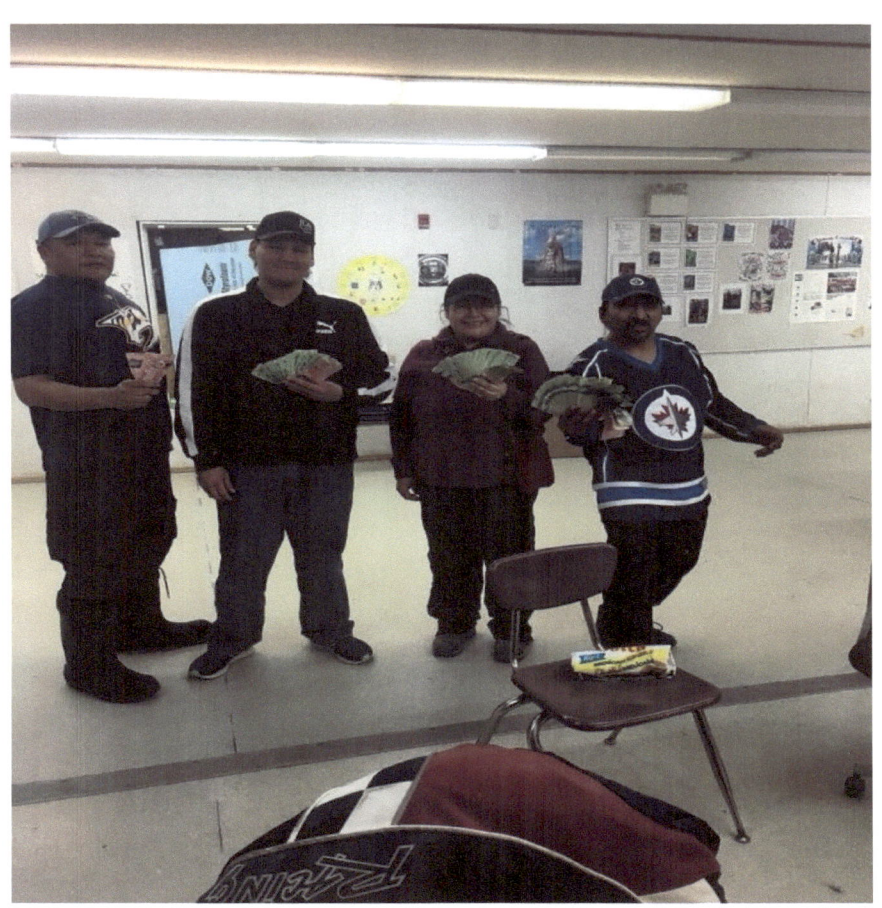

Cousins
Nichesanak oko eskewak asisikapowechik

Daughters and grand-daughter

Nichanisak ekwa nosesim

Daughters, son, nephews, grandkids

Nechanisak ekwa nikosis, nitotemak, ekwa nosisimak

www.ingramcontent.com/pod-product-compliance
Lightning Source LLC
Chambersburg PA
CBHW041227040426
42444CB00002B/75